GREEN GOLD ANIMATION PVT. LTD.

PRESENTS

CHHOTA BHEEM ™ VOL. 66

in

alibaba's cave

Created By: Rajiv Chilaka

Story: Nidhi Anand

One day two robbers who are the descendents of the famous Ali Baba and the Forty thieves come to Dholakpur. They become emotional after eating Tuntun aunty's Laddoos and ask her to make ten baskets full of Laddoos and bring it to them everyday. Meanwhile Kalia tries to help her and takes the cart to the robbers. He becomes greedy midway and eats one full basket of Laddoos. The thieves find out that they have been cheated and kidnap Tuntun aunty and Kalia. Will Bheem be able to save Tuntun aunty, Kalia and his favourite Laddoos? Read this fascinating story of Ali Baba's Cave, filled with mystery and adventure.

Bheem, a nine-year-old boy, is brave, strong, intelligent, adventurous and fun loving. Bheem loves food especially laddoos and bananas. He becomes stronger than his usual self when he eats his favourite - laddoos. Even though only a kid, Bheem is stronger than most men and is always there to protect the poor and needy.

Chutki is a seven-year-old girl, who is simple, graceful and intelligent. She is Bheem's closest friend, and loves to accompany Bheem in his adventures and helps him in the good deeds he does. She even helps him eat laddoos from her mother's sweet shop. Everybody loves Chutki for her generous, sweet and happy nature.

Raju is a cute, small, four-year-old boy, who totally looks up to Bheem and considers him to be his ideal hero. Raju is extremely brave and tough for his age (like Arjuna) and is one of the very few children who is not afraid of Kalia Pahelwan. Raju's father is a soldier in the King's army and he dreams of becoming the General some day. He loves playing war games, especially the game where Bheem is the 'King' and he, the 'General'.

Jaggu is Bheem's pet monkey and friend. He is a talking monkey and is of great help to Bheem, especially, when they are in the Jungle. He always supports Bheem and accompanies him in all his adventures. Jaggu is a clever and funny little monkey who has a great sense of humour. He loves playing tricks on Dholu, Bholu and Kalia. All the children adore Jaggu because he always entertains them.

Kalia is a ten-year-old boy, who is bulky and strong. As he is jealous of Bheem's popularity and strength, Kalia always tries to make Bheem look bad and tries to land him in trouble. He picks on children younger and weaker than him to prove his superiority. He has two silly followers, Dholu and Bholu, who either help him in his plans or completely abandon him.

Dholu & Bholu are the cowardly followers of Kalia Pahelwan. They are identical twin brothers who dress and behave alike. Dholu and Bholu are extremely dumb and keep getting into awfully silly situations. Occasionally, they allow themselves to be bribed by Chutki's laddoos and are therefore not always loyal to Kalia – inspite of his repeated threats.

IT'S A LOVELY MORNING IN DHOLAKPUR. THE BREEZE IS BEAUTIFUL; THE SKY IS IMMENSELY BLUE WITH WHITE SILVERY CLOUDS AND THE MARKET PLACE LOOKED BUSY AND LIVELY AS USUAL

AS THE SHOPKEEPERS OPENED THEIR SHOPS...

...TWO STRANGERS MAKE THEIR WAY TOWARDS A FRUIT SHOP

HMPH!?

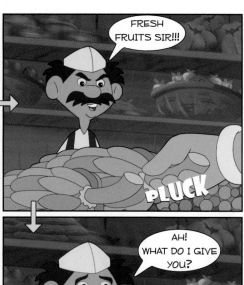

FRESH FRUITS SIR!!!

PLUCK

AH! WHAT DO I GIVE YOU?

TWEAK

THE TWO MEN IGNORE THE SHOP KEEPER AND START EATING

MUNCH

CHOMP

ALRIGHT SIR, NOW PLEASE PAY ONE RUPEE EACH FOR THE FRUITS!

WHAT DID YOU SAY? ONLY ONE RUPEE?

WELL, YES SIR!

HERE IS ONE...

...AND TWO

EHHH!

THE VILLAGERS ARE SHOCKED TO SEE THEM BEHAVE LIKE THAT

UH!

OH NO!!!

DO YOU WANT SOME MORE?

HA HA HA!

AAHHH!

THEY START ATTACKING THE PEOPLE...

...AND CREATE NUISANCE ALL OVER THE...

RUN

...MARKET PLACE

GET LOST OR ELSE WE WILL BASH YOU!

IS THAT CLEAR?

KICK

PEOPLE RAN AWAY...

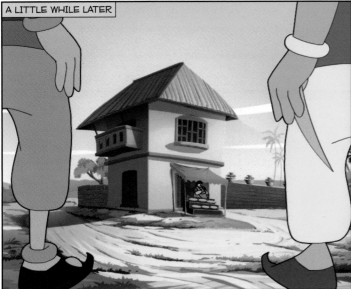

RUN!

HEY BROTHER, RUN FASTER!

...AND SOON THE MARKET PLACE LOOKED DESERTED

HA! HA!

HA! HA! HA!

A LITTLE WHILE LATER

SHOO... GOD THESE FLIES!

BUZZ

BUZZ

BOO HOO!!
MUMMY!!

PUFF

YIKES!

OH!
HE LOOKS SO
HAPPY!

HMMM...
DELICIOUS!

BUT...
WHO ARE YOU?
NEVER SEEN YOU
HERE BEFORE!

HEY, HAVE YOU
HEARD THE TALE OF
ALI BABA AND THE FORTY
THIEVES?

OF COURSE
YES... ARE YOU
ALI BABA?

NO... NO,
WE ARE THE FORTY
THIEVES!

HA! HA! HA!

HA! HA!
HA!

HUH? BUT THAT IS AN OLD STORY NOW!

HOW ON EARTH ARE YOU THE FORTY THIEVES?

WELL, WE ARE THE DESCENDANTS OF THOSE FORTY THIEVES!

UH!?

HA HA HA! FOOLISH WOMAN

BUT WE MUST ADMIT THAT YOU MAKE THE FINEST LADDOOS...

...AND MUST BE REWARDED

WOW!!!

OKAY, FROM TODAY ONWARDS IT IS DECIDED THAT...

I WONDER WHAT THE REWARD IS GOING TO BE!

TUNTUN AUNTY ANXIOUSLY WAITS TO HEAR WHAT THE ROBBERS HAVE TO SAY

COME ON TELL ME!

YOU WILL MAKE TEN BASKETS OF LADDOOS, FOR ALL OF US...

...AND THAT TOO FOR FREE!

HUH!?

I HOPE MOTHER DOES NOT SEE ME!

HEY, CHUTKI!

AAH!!! BHEEM!

I AM SURE CHUTKI WILL GET LADDOOS FOR ME!

THANK GOD!!! AUNTY DID NOT SEE CHUTKI!

JUST THEN

CAUGHT YOU!!!

AH!!!

DON'T YOU DARE TAKE A SINGLE PIECE OF LADDOO!

TCK!!! TCK!!!

MY DEAR, YOU ARE NOT AWARE WHAT THEY WILL DO, IF ALL THE TEN BASKETS OF...

HUH!?

10

...LADDOOS DO NOT REACH THE ROBBERS!

SOB! SOB! SOB!

OH MOTHER, PLEASE DON'T CRY!

CHUTKI FEELS VERY BAD FOR HER MOTHER AND TELLS HER FRIENDS ABOUT THE ROBBERS

CHUTKI! DON'T LOOK SO WORRIED!

HMMM... I UNDERSTAND THAT THIS IS A SERIOUS PROBLEM!

OH NO!!! BUT HOW CAN WE LIVE WITHOUT LADDOOS?

BUT MOTHER CANNOT ESCAPE FROM THIS NOW

IS IT SO?

YES, THOSE ROBBERS HAVE THREATENED AND WARNED HER!

DON'T WORRY CHUTKI, WE WILL SOON THINK OF SOMETHING TO CAPTURE THE ROBBERS!

HUH!!! HOW ARE LADDOOS CONNECTED TO THIEVES?

MEANWHILE KALIA WITH HIS MINIONS HEARS THE CONVERSATION

UH!

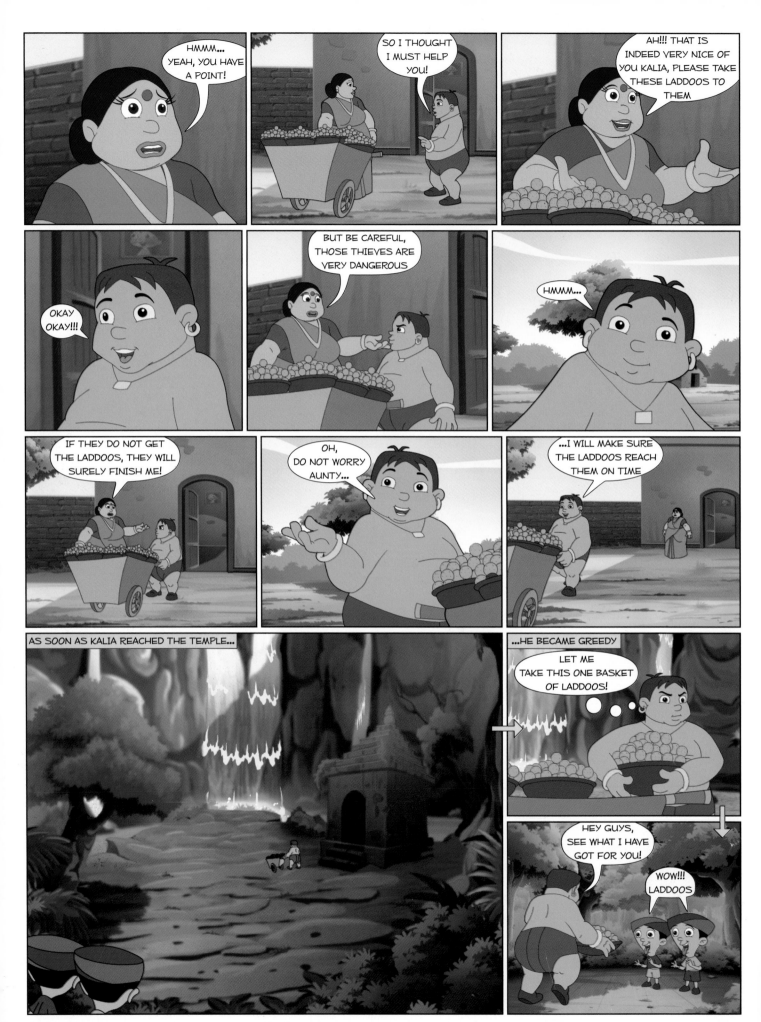

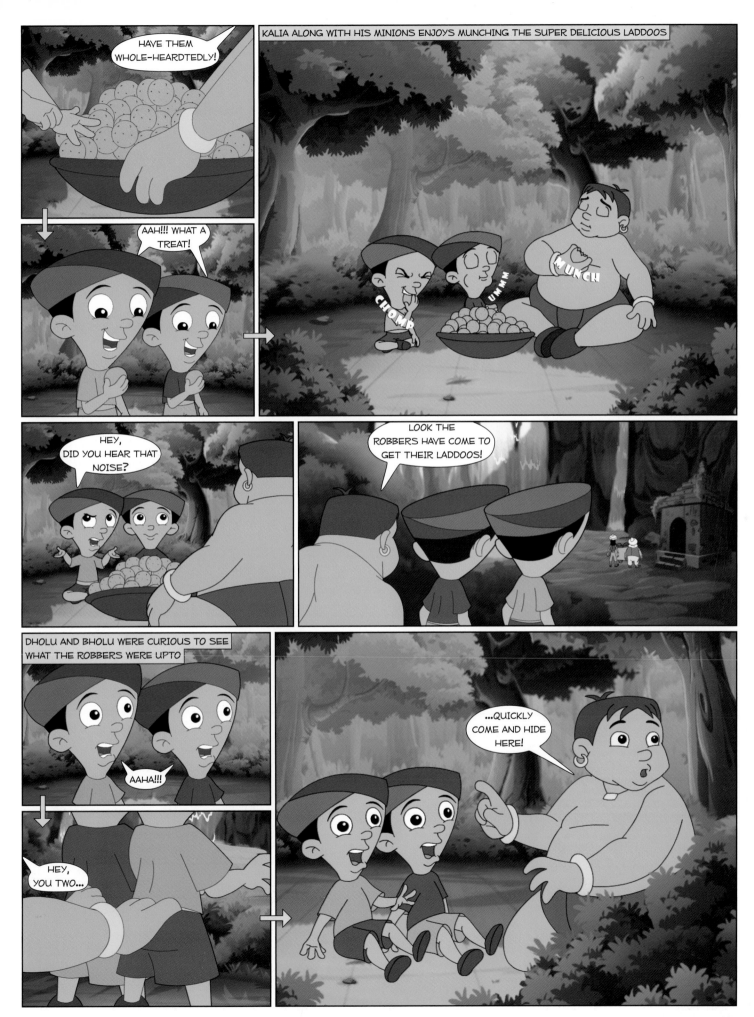

THE ROBBERS ARE VERY DELIGHTED TO SEE THE CART FULL OF LADDOOS

HA HA HA! HERE IS OUR YUMMY BREAKFAST!

FIRST LET US MAKE SURE THAT NO ONE IS WATCHING US!

WAIT, I WILL LOOK AROUND AND SEE!

DON'T WORRY, NO ONE IS IN SIGHT...

...COME ON NOW GET THE BASKETS INSIDE THE CAVE!

OH!?

UH!?

SOON THE ROBBER USES A SECRET CODE TO ENTER INTO THE CAVE

OPEN SIM SIM!

AS YOU WISH, MASTER

THE CAVE WAS A DEEP HOLLOW PASSAGE WITH A VERY HIGH ROOF

COME LET US GO!

DHOLU AND BHOLU COME RUNNING TO BHEEM AND NARRATE THE ENTIRE STORY

WHAT ARE YOU GUYS TALKING ABOUT?

ARE YOU SURE WHATEVER YOU ARE SAYING IS TRUE?

YES, BHEEM! AND NOW KALIA HAS GONE INSIDE THE CAVE ALL ALONE...

HUH!?

JUST THEN A MAN HURRIEDLY COMES THERE

HEY! BHEEM, CHUTKI! BAD NEWS...

...TO GET HIS HANDS ON THE TREASURE!

EH!?

UNCLE, WHAT IS THE MATTER?

THOSE THIEVES HAVE TAKEN TUNTUN SISTER WITH THEM...

...AND THEY ARE VERY ANGRY...

WHAT???

...AND WERE SAYING THAT SHE WOULD BE PUNISHED FOR THAT!

PUNISHED FOR WHAT?

I HEARD THEM SAYING THAT THEY RECEIVED LESS NUMBER OF LADDOOS

LESS LADDOOS? BUT THAT IS NOT POSSIBLE

OH!

MOTHER HAD SENT TEN BASKETS FULL OF LADDOOS TO THEM!

HEARING CHUTKI, DHOLU AND BHOLU REVEAL THE TRUTH

ERR... KALIA AND WE, ON THE WAY TO THE CAVE...

...UM...UH.. ATE SOME...

...OF THE LADDOOS!

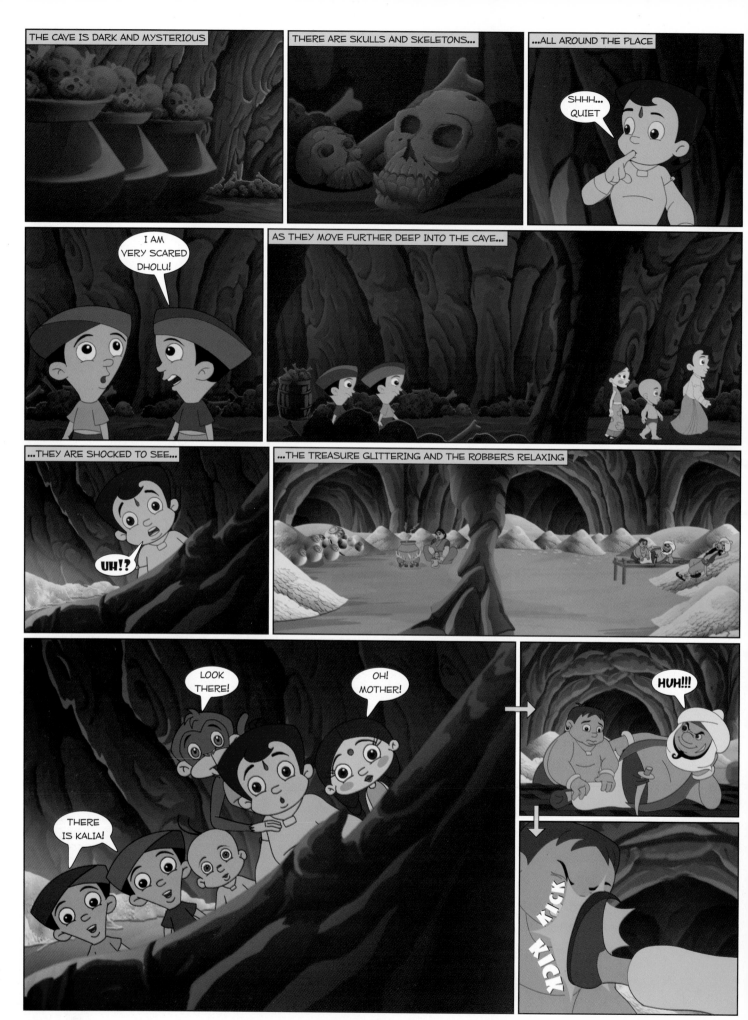

HELP TUNTUN AUNTY CHASE KALIA TILL THE END

CHHOTA BHEEM COMIC BOOKS

Special Edition

Special Edition

PATALIPUTRA
(Rs.199/-)

MAYANAGARI
(Rs.249/-)

Special Edition

Movie Edition

DHOLAKPUR TO KATHMANDU
(Rs.249/-)

CHHOTA BHEEM AND
THE CURSE OF DAMYAAN
(Rs.249/-)